Never Be the Same

Gwen Hart

FUTURECYCLE PRESS
www.futurecycle.org

Cover artwork, NightCafe spin on U. Lucas Dubé-Cantin's "Fox Near Grass" by Diane Kistner; cover and interior design by Diane Kistner; Adobe Garamond Pro text and titling

Library of Congress Control Number: 2022950016

Published by FutureCycle Press
Athens, Georgia, USA

ISBN 978-1-952593-46-8

for Roger, upon whom the plot depends

Contents

I.
Endangered Species

II.
The Hard Way

III.
They Said It Couldn't Be Done

IV.
Never Be the Same

V.
Watching the Fox Disappear

I.

Endangered Species

The Easy-Bake Oven Presages Disappointment

when it appears
my seventh Christmas,
its heart an ordinary
100-watt light bulb
unscrewed from the fixture
above the kitchen sink—
I am crestfallen
it is not a real
miniaturized oven
as seen on TV.
By summer, the tiny pans
are lined up at the top
of the backyard metal slide
and filled with mud
pies baking in the sun.
The plastic oven shell
tilts in the back of the closet,
a discarded Barbie doll
sticking out the door.
*Maybe you won't want
things like that anymore,*
predicts my mother. Maybe
I will want them more.

We Loved Them, and She Didn't

One Saturday in 1985, my mother refused
to drive us to the gas station convenience store
to buy Garbage Pail Kids cards to trade
at school. *They're disgusting,*
she complained, pointing to Brainy Jane's
cracked-open skull and Clogged Duane
screaming as he was sucked down the drain.
She failed to see the value in purpled Varicose Wayne
or Handy Randy reaching his fingers through his face
to wiggle them like teeth inside his open mouth.
There was no place in our house, she explained,
for Tom Tom, who twisted off his own head
in order to beat it bloody like a drum.
She didn't understand that to get through
the ugliness of childhood, to swim—not sink—
like Potty Scotty, to survive, against all odds,
like Oozy Suzy, whose wax head, tipped
with a lit wick, melted and ran hot down
the length of her body, or Adam Bomb, whose crown
exploded into a bright orange mushroom cloud,
was an excruciating task, made easier
if there were someone to laugh at,
someone like Jack Splat, printed flat
on a trading card, with a cartoon grin,
missing teeth, and green snot on his face—
someone *not* you, not even *real,* but still
your very own, to keep, to trade, to tear in half,
to shout at—*Aw, gross!*—as a spout of guts
ruptured across the paper, and you bled
all of your feelings out, and slid them carefully
into a three-ring binder with clear plastic sleeves—
three faces to a line, three lines to a page,
smoothing down the emptiness, the loneliness,
the loathing, and the rage.

Endangered Species

While riding the yellow school bus,
we pretended we were anywhere else—
a castle on wheels, or a cliff dwelling
with the high windows we weren't allowed
to open or stick our heads out of. Billy Brown
got up early for his stop and yelled *Surf's up!*,
throwing out his arms and balancing
down the aisle as the bus shuddered
to a halt. As soon as he hopped off
and rode a wave down his driveway,
we were plunged into prickly pear
country, full of rattlesnakes and sagebrush.
It seemed less dangerous than where
we were headed—the den where Dad
added maraschino cherries to his fourth
cocktail, or the bedroom where mom had
the blankets pulled over her head,
or the yellow kitchen where Grandma
was burning waffles because she thought
it was morning, not evening, again.
The bus made its loop in reverse,
so the first to be picked up in the morning
were the last to be dropped off.
Our numbers dwindled until
there were only a few of us left clinging
to the green vinyl seats, an endangered
species winding our way through
the wilds of suburbia, huddled inside
our moving imaginations.

Make Your Anxiety Work for You

Thin as a shadow,
she masters *tripod-*
headstand-tripod-
roll for third grade
gym class by wearing a path
in the grass in the backyard,
and, when it rains,
crushing the maroon
carpet in the family room
with the crown of her head,
elbows, and knees.
Triumphant, she decides
to stick by your side
forever. When you can't sleep,
you balance on your toes
on one side
of the metal daybed frame,
she perches on the other,
and you somersault
through each other,
trading places
all night long.

Your Anxiety Takes You to the Half-Price Movie Theater

You sneak in bags of stale popcorn and boxes of Junior Mints
from the dime store at the end of the plaza, hug

the bulky sleeves of your coats, hustle past
the glass eye of the assistant manager.

There's never anything good playing,
just the leftovers from the mall's movie megaplex,

but you are already good Americans at age eleven,
and getting a bargain is better than discovering

a pirate's buried treasure. You suck on Lemonheads
and grin sideways in the dark. You relish the sugar crash

after the credits roll, tongues glued to the roofs of your mouths,
two girls giggling in the broken stalls of the women's restroom.

You are amazed that, after the fanged clowns,
car chases, gun battles, and exploding villages,

you can walk out the cracked glass doors
onto the street-lit sidewalk and race each other

across the abandoned fairgrounds, past the hog barn
and the craft palace, and back to your mother's well-lit house,

neither of you outpacing the other.

Everything Is Corn

Everything is corn. —2016 Ethanol Producers Slogan

Even the weeds in the neighbor's garden are corn,
green leaves spiraling up, thick and insistent.
The most likely suspect, third from the left
in any ingredient list—*high fructose corn syrup.*
The dog's nose twitching in its sleep is purple
corn working toward a peak in a time-lapse
recording, the worm shimmering on the sidewalk
is corn gone soft and mealy. The kinked fingers
of the girl clinging to the monkey bars, knuckles
white with strain, and her mother's corn silk hair
shimmering in the sunlight as she cheers the girl on,
the color of the equal sign dividing
one lane of traffic from the other—all of it is pure corn,
golden, red, or white, boiled up and buttery,
dried in the husk, dent corn, flint corn, pod corn,
popcorn, flour corn, and sweet corn, poured in the bin,
pulverized into ethanol, flattened into tortillas or rolled
into batter for corn dogs at the state fair. In Iowa, we take
corn seriously, plant it all the way up to the edge
of the road, stop signs be damned, hang it
on our front doors come autumn, the fields stripped
to a brown stubble the crows pick over. We nail it
above our welcome mats like a talisman,
a hunk of the real to shield us from the tall corn
of our dreams, that white, sweet elusive corn that falls
apart like loose teeth when we reach for it.

Post-Madonna, I Tried Not to Look Afraid

They said it would make me feel better.
I couldn't just leave it there, blowing bubbles in the surf.
I took it in because of my upbringing.
I took it easily, with one finger pressed to my chin.
I folded it into my skin.
It was the color of the sky in Iowa in July.
I took it in 1987, 1988, and 1989.
It was the only shell on the empty beach.
I felt as thin and cloudy as waxed paper.
It curled up in my hand like a fiddlehead.
I posed, a material girl, arms akimbo.

What's Missing

I love Lake Geneva!
shrieks a woman on the street
who grabs me by the arm
and shakes me. I have never
been to Lake Geneva,
but I've been to the Goodwill
where I ransacked the $1 T-shirt rack
and came out with a folded
rainbow, including
this emerald green T-shirt:
Life Is Good, Lake Geneva.

Did you ride the mailboat?
the woman demands, giving my arm
another shake, and I have no idea
what she is talking about,
but as she goes on about
how wonderful summers
in Lake Geneva are, I vaguely recall
a news story about a community
in Wisconsin where teenagers
make daring leaps on and off
a small ferry to deliver mail.

I thought I was walking
around town wearing
a T-shirt born in Geneva,
Switzerland, a cast-off from
a mysteriously wealthy neighbor,
but Wisconsin makes sense
since I am, in fact, in Iowa,
where a woman has just
given up trying to shake
some sense into me.

Later, my husband demands
to know what my red T-shirt
that reads *Master of Karate*
and Friendship for Everyone

is supposed to mean. It really
seems to tick him off. In the
center of the shirt, a figure
in silhouette executes a perfect
horizontal kick while lines
of power radiate around him—
or her. *I don't know,* I say,
maybe it's a joke?

And the blue shirt I try not to wear
outside at all because I am so tired
of trying to explain it reads,
There are two types of people
in this world: 1. Those who can
extrapolate from incomplete data.

What's missing can't be found
here, can be only partially printed
on any T-shirt, and I am wearing
these slogans the same way I am wandering
through this life, salvaging
the bright puzzle pieces, assembling
and reassembling them
in the kaleidoscope of each new day.

II.
The Hard Way

Oh, Are You Supposed to Use a Knife?

It was like thumbing
out the hearts of small animals,
splitting the red meat
and peeling out the bones—
slippery—cherry juice
squirting all over
the countertop, the cookbook,
your fingers until you yelled,
Get me some paper towels,
stat, and only after the towels
and your palms, cuticles,
knuckles, wrists
and elbows were stained
crimson and ember and plum,
the pits on a paper plate
and the pulp piled
up high in the bowl,
all the life squeezed
out of it, only then
did you wonder.

Rest Area Outside Des Moines

John, consulting his iPhone,
says it could be
a very rare albino,
but more likely,
it's a piebald
with a tiny patch
of brown somewhere
on its underbelly.

The fading sun paints
the white deer
yellow and red.

I start to ask what
difference it makes
what we call it,
but Cheryl is digging
her camera out of
the backseat. She fiddles
with the telephoto lens
and curses God
for dead batteries.

My left foot wobbles
in my denim wedges.

One in 30,000, recites John,
still reading statistics
from the screen.

My fingers itch
and stiffen. My grip
on my purse strap loosens.

What are you doing? cries Cheryl
when I crouch on all fours.

But I don't answer her.
My ears twitch, and I
spring over the barbed wire
fence and sprint
into the glow.

What Gets to Me

Not the flatland, but the wind.
Not the kernel, but the cob.
Not the turbine, but the spin.
Not the cattle, but the prod.

Not the train, but the whistle.
Not the gravel, but the road.
Not the flower, but the thistle.
Not the semi, but the load.

Not the prairie, but the weeds.
Not the lightning, but the bug.
Not the berry, but the seeds.
Not the milk, but the jug.

Not the quilting, but the needle.
Not the dog, but the bark.
Not the dung, but the beetle.
Not the stars, but the dark.

Drop Risk

I thought it meant being at risk
of dropping something
like a heavy wrench
from a great height,
a tall scaffolding,
but, no, my diesel students
explain, *It's when you're working*
on an oil pipeline and you're
standing in six inches
of muddy water and
you could get electrocuted!
Oh, I say, *so it's you*
who's going to drop.
As an English professor,
I have not worried much
about this risk, but
when I peer into the boiler room
of Cowan Hall—the door open
directly across from my classroom—
I can hear the maintenance crew
discussing yet another problem
with the heating system,
even though I can't see them
for the vast and intricate duct work,
like a maze, with multiple-storied
catwalks, and I am shocked
by this world that exists parallel
to my own, branching out,
as complex as a Victorian novel,
full of electric secrets and long,
frayed lines of disappointment, sparking,
just there, on the other side of the wall.

Re: Meetings

The meeting will start at 4:13 sharp.
Bring your laptop, ID badge, three unvarnished pinecones,
and one jagged shard of glass. Meetings will be held alternate Wednesdays,
second Fridays, odd Tuesdays, and all Mondays, rain or shine.
Morning meetings will involve mourning the results
of earlier meetings. Afternoon meetings will be held underground.
Meetings are essential to our progress as longer
daylight hours are essential to the petunia seeds' sprouting.
If forty-seven of us are in a room, the meetings will have meetings.
The female cardinal and the male cardinal cross paths
under the crabapple tree without meeting.
You are required to take notes with the pointed end
of a seashell dipped in melted snow at every meeting.
In the film, the camera panned slowly through
the crowd to show two lovers' eyes meeting.
You have been appointed to figure out the point
of the meeting in Ballroom A. Can you feel your heart beating,
meeting after meeting? If there is not enough seating, you will stand
and be grateful. When this meeting concludes, please proceed
down the hall to your left and into the next meeting.

Marriage Poem

I love
it when

my husband
turns on

the windshield
wipers instead

of the
headlights or

trips over
the rug

or forgets
all of

his secret
computer passwords

because then
I know

we are
walking this

road in
tandem.

Your Anxiety Books a VRBO

She is thrilled and terrified
to be in someone else's house,
where she moves silently
from room to room
as if someone is listening.
She isn't interested in
the view, but spends hours
sitting in the closets,
smelling the cracked board games
and touching the frayed sleeves
of windbreakers. She slides
under the bed, inhaling the dust
and dog hair. She takes all
the mismatched pots and pans
out of the cupboards beneath
the kitchen counter,
crawls in, and stretches out, segmented
like the beautiful assistant
in a magician's show,
head in one cabinet,
feet in another,
and falls asleep
on the sticky wood
to the sound of mice
gnawing on the supports
underneath the floorboards.

2020

Walking
along the riverbank
we find
offerings
of dead fish
the water deposits
here and there
on the sand
as if to say,
This is how
to mourn,
and when
you can't
mourn anymore,
this is how
to move on.

Your Anxiety Crushes on Donald Sutherland's Character in *Backdraft*

She adores his sideways grin,
singsong dialogue, and the way
his mustache twists to the left
when he talks dreamily
about setting fires.
How easy it is to be kindling!
Every time her heart is broken,
she is a love letter crumpled
in the wastebasket,
sprayed with Rave hairspray,
and inflected with sparks
until only *Dear* and ashes
remain. She is always looking
for a place to douse her heart.
Rainbows of gasoline!
Rainbows of oil!
She remembers when Cleveland
set the Cuyahoga River on fire
just to spruce it up
for a party. She won't share
the flint she's fingering
in her pocket.
You want her to go,
so she goes up in flames,
from the tips of her eyelashes
to the cloud of her
bright orange mane.

III.

They Said It Couldn't Be Done

They Said It Couldn't Be Done

We were in our old kitchen:
You were you, and I was the vegetable peeler.
I peeled carrots for you,
long strings of orange longing,
but you were too distracted.
I peeled cucumbers,
sparing the sweet white
flesh and taking only
the hard, waxy rind.
I wanted you to put more
vinegar in the dressing.
You were wearing a yellow
flowered apron and singing
the wrong words to "Pink Houses."
I wanted to tell you that if it had to be
John Cougar Mellencamp, "Hurts so Good"
was a better choice. But my lips
were two razor blades angled to slice
skin from bone. If I could only
press my sharpest self
against your lips, maybe
an eyebrow. Your new girlfriend
was trying to peel an apple
with me. I wanted to scream.
She's an idiot, you know. She made you
give up cheese. Is lactose intolerance
catching? Later, I heard
you two in the other room, spooning
on the couch like lettuce leaves,
and I wanted to hurl myself
head-first down the garbage disposal.
In the morning, as you tried
to put me back in the drawer,
I got you, took a small hunk
out of your ring finger,
and you bled.

I Used to Be a Roller Coaster Girl,

a spoiled child. My eyes have seen
what my heart has felt. The body remembers
hunger, love songs, what it's like to have
nothing to do, to shout *Now what?*
letting the emptiness become my government.

*

At night, five moths in the gloaming,
in the roiling night, the changing light.
I never figured out how to get free
of the lap belt, to say *I am a hummingbird,*
to be a meadowlark, be make-believe.

*

Will you say a prayer severing the circle,
a prayer on joy and sorrow, on anger,
on Jakarta, January, a prayer for the youth
of Florence, Kentucky, for all
the inevitable just-about-to-break-out
sounds in the fragmentary blue?

*

We are all waiting for answers,
for a louder thing at the grave of the forgotten,
so many untitled names: Dear Nainai,
Dear Deliliah! I imagine each woman—I picture her lips
are copper wires; her hair is a petting zoo;
her heart is a trumpet.

*

Half girl, then elegy, somewhere deep in the cell,
in the mortal lease, there is a war within myself.
In the final loop-de-loop, I can see this much
and more—triple moments of light
and industry, one geography of belonging,
of color, of landscape, of tenuous rope.

—Poem welded together from 47 titles from Poem-a-Day 2019

Your Anxiety Joins the Cast of SNL

She isn't actually written
into any skit, so she makes
her own magic. She pulls
a lampshade down over
her face and stands
behind the couch on the suburban
family room set. You can
just make out her eyes
sparking above
the married couple's heads.
Their paranoia about the neighbors
watching them feels real.
She wraps herself in aluminum foil
and crinkles along the mirror
at the back of the gymnasium scene,
warping the actors' reflections
as they confess how much they hate
their thighs, the flesh of their armpits.
She crawls on her hands
and knees under the white linen
tablecloth in the fancy restaurant
breakup skit, banging into
the man's shins and giving
his anger during the fight scene
a wounded edge. You glimpse
her again in the final
live moments of the show,
flapping her arms frantically
at the periphery of the crowd,
high-fiving herself
over and over again.

To My Children

You're zeroes, goose eggs, blanks on every form.
You'll never be cursed, never be kissed
goodbye, never twist up your faces and fists,
never yell, "I hate you, Mom!"

You can't be quantified. You resist
speculation. You'll never raise alarm;
never rage or curse. A kiss goodnight, the kiss
of death—it's all the same to you. The apocalypse
is just another day you won't be, *can't* be harmed.

When people tell me all the joy I've missed,
I think of you, and I feel wholly calm.
You'll never need. Never be cursed—or kissed—

by lovers. You won't feel a thing, blessed and bodiless.
Darlings, this is my curse; this is my kiss.

I Was Not Raised to Expect Miracles

Shuddering around the back field,
        kicking and twisting,
                rejecting rootedness,

the tumbleweed banked
        against the fence
                and turned, wild-haired,

levitating, revealing
        a fine lacing of brambles,
                then dropped like a bird's nest

over the barbed wire.
        Upended again, it swung
                sideways, cupped the air,

poked at the wind
        with its crooked fingers,
                almost unspooling,

turning belly-up,
        so that it rose
                like a hot air balloon's

wicker basket high
        into the sky. I shouted
                after it, but my voice

was just a string clipped
        from a kite. I could
                no more call it back

than I could join
        it in flight, the dust
                lifting and settling

around my ankles.

Rabbit Logic

How many times
have I built a nest
under a bush in a fenced yard,
only to be threatened
by a dog's angry maw?

Or followed finch logic,
tussling with another finch
over the red berries in the tree,
when there are enough
on the branches for
a dozen more?

Some days, like the chipmunk,
I snap off the tender
sunflower sprouts
as soon as they appear,
instead of harvesting
a whole winter's stockpile
of seeds in the fall.

Then, one with the gopher,
I tunnel escape routes
in every direction,
so the first spring storm fills
my burrow with rain.

I pray I can be like the owl
on the fence post, biding
my time, imagining
each detail—cocked ear,
furred foot, fine whisker,
such craftsmanship!—the hare
that will surely dart out
of the shadows any
minute, any minute now.

Your Anxiety Visits Liam Neeson in His Future Rest Home

Allison, are you saying I'm too f------ old to be acting, is that what you're getting at? Come on, tell me the truth. —Liam Neeson in an interview in *AARP Magazine*, 2022

She approaches him carefully,
with fresh lipstick,
tousled hair,
and her best
I-could-be-kidnapped look.
He is not having what
the nurse's aides call
a *good day*.
He tried to kill two orderlies
before breakfast—put one in a choke hold
and thrust a shish kebob stick
meant for melting marshmallows
toward the center of another's eye.

Your anxiety removes
the bathroom mirror
to show him there is
no bomb ticking there,
and checks his roommate's
oxygen tank to make sure
it is not rigged with a detonator.

When he continues
to insist *We're running
out of time!* she nods knowingly,
puts a slim finger to her lips,
and whispers that he must
keep up his cover a little longer,
here among the dentures
and hot water bottles.

She must convince him
that staying under the radar
will save her fragile, blonde life.
She pats his swollen knuckles,

stiff with arthritis from punching out
the fire alarm, and his left knee,
which buckles when he tries to kick
an attendant with the right.

She is lying, of course,
she is in no danger,
but she knows what it means
to be unwanted,
to be told you've *lost the plot,*
while, all around you, the smallest
signs, from the bleating alarm
at the nurses' station
to the movie poster taped to the wall
pull you in to dark fantasies
where only you
can save the world.

Ode to the Geode

Clod of storm
cloud; hoard
of the head
toad's treasure;
hailstone for any
weather; crumb
of angel dung;
egg pulled
from the dregs
of fairy tales;
desiccated
dream; prehistoric
plaything; center
of a Cyclops's
forehead; devil's
eight ball; petrified
drum roll; folded
reef; ball of spiky
inner grief;
secret that never
melts, no matter
how tightly held;
barnacle-encrusted
bell; mouth cracked
open in a silent yell.

IV.

Never Be the Same

The Quaint Seaside Village Will Never Be the Same

Watch enough BBC television,
and you begin to question your sanity:
I know this guy, he's a murderer! No, wait,
he's a cop! No, now he's a priest! How could they
let him be a cop and a priest after he killed
all those people in that quaint seaside village?

You start to notice the same phenomenon
in real life. It's harmless enough—
The new postal carrier looks like the old
grocery store clerk, minus the apron and plus
a blue hat and pants. The shaggy, bearded
man hunched at the dock once played
a broad-shouldered football star
in an after-school special, right before
he went off to war in that acclaimed miniseries.

Your parents fought; they made up. Your childhood
was a sitcom. Now, some days you barely
recognize them. Your mother dyes her hair
red, goes back to school and becomes
an accountant. They split up,
and your father offers you scotch
in his girlfriend's Ft. Lauderdale condo.
When you confront them, they shrug.
What do you want from us? We were young.
We took the roles we could get.

Shopping at the Goodwill in your white T-shirt
and dark jeans, a lacy green dress
from an Edwardian love story calls
to you, and, for two dollars, how can you afford
not to try it on? You pull the dress down over
your clothes, then catch your reflection
winking at you from the mirror. Her eyes are wide,
and there's something twitchy about her mouth.
Her hair has come loose from its ponytail,
and flares out above her shoulders, kinked
by the beveled edges of the glass.

You back into a dark-haired man
with a caramel-colored suit jacket slung
over his shoulder who reminds you of a skinny boy
in a striped shirt from two rows over
in high school calculus. But really, he could be anyone,
from any time or place—you won't know what
scene you're in until he looks you in the eye
and offers the opening lines. The electricity
you feel when he offers his hand tells you,
no matter the plot, you'll be hooked
for the whole season, waiting week
after week for a new episode
to wash over you, to drag you under.

The Devil's Kettle

Two roads diverged in a yellow wood,
And sorry I could not travel both
And be one traveler, long I stood...

—Robert Frost

In June, the waterfall breaks through
the ice of indecision and chooses
all of the above. The rocks are as efficient
as a tailor with his scissors, cutting
the waterfall neatly in two, letting one leg down,
and pinning the other up tight, like a white
handkerchief a magician pushes
back up his sleeve. The water falls
everywhere and nowhere, rushing
to explore two paths at once. Standing
at the lower falls and looking up
at the intricate rockwork, people murmur
or watch in silence, flat stones, plants trembling
leaf by leaf in the mist. Like Robert Johnson,
the river must have made a deal
with the devil to take its music
in so many directions: a chipped enamel
washtub poured out; a white, starchy torrent
of rain; an earth-bound comet, rich as heavy cream.
It needs no audience but the blackberries,
runs day and night, breathless, the paint
brimming the container, sloshing everywhere,
doubling itself into twin travelers
with no passports, suitcases flung
over a cliff, white shirts and rumpled
nightclothes tumbling collar over ruffle
over hem, all joy, all encore, a torrent
of *yesses* overpowering every *no.*

You Bring Out the Klimt in Me

the long red hair,
edge of the meadow
in me. The flowered crown,
curled toes, hanging-on-for-dear-life
in me. The all-seeing
dress, bare breasts,
crooked neck, modern woman
in me. You bring me
outside of me. You bring out
the intertwined arms
and legs in me,
the peacock pattern,
lemon yellow,
gold leaf in me. You wheel
out the stars in me
and the sunflowers,
bright petals high
as the crown of a tree,
dark leaves kissing.
I walk the mottled
garden path.
The brown chickens
cluck, the hollyhocks
sway. The table
under the arbor
is meant for two.
I will curve
to any canvas
you choose.

Isn't It Something?

What is it in my face, my hair, my walk
that's reminiscent of Harriet, Genevieve, or Ruth?
All the old men want to stop and talk

about their sweethearts, the ones they shared malts
with, or their sisters' friends, who soothed
their hurts somehow. My face, my hair, my walk

are ordinary, but still, they stop and gawk.
You look just like her—Mary, from Duluth!
It's always old men. When they stop and talk,

their eyes light up with warmth and shock,
as if they've found the lost fountain of youth.
Isn't it something? My face, my hair, my walk

are scrutinized. What is it that's unlocked
the past? Then, *I know you can't be her*—the proof
so clear, so cruel it stops them in their tracks,

the ever-present ticking of the clock.
Finally, I recognize the truth:
It isn't something in my face, my hair, my walk,
but—I'm the only one who'll stop and talk.

Goldfinches

The sunflower,
heavy with seeds,
but still ringed
with yellow,
snaps upright
when the petals
take flight!

Falling Letters

Pumpkins thrown
from a blue pickup
can't be scraped up
whole. They wait
in the road, envelopes
of seeds in the
dead letter office.

A bevy of apples
from the other side
of the lake
bobs playfully—
Return to Sender.

A maple leaf
carried *par avion*
and pressed flat
against my cheek
has red palm
lines too delicate
to read.

Tiny missives of rain
precede the snow.
The dog seals
autumn with his paw
pressed hard
through the last
of this year's mud.

Seven Monks, Bodh Gaya, India

—after a photograph by Swasti Bhattacharyya

The bell rings twice. Because the bell is hollow,
the tongue is free to move and make this sign.
Wherever silence goes, reflection follows.

The monks are still. They sit through rain in rows,
in tune with falling raindrops and their minds.
The bell rings twice because the bell is hollow,

signaling the end of meditation's flow.
The monks rise up and walk along a line
wherever silence goes. Reflection follows

them along the winding path. Their slow
progress, barefoot, echoes the peace they find.
The bell rings twice because the bell is hollow;

it holds its tone in sunlight and in shadow.
The monks are quiet. They keep their steps aligned.
Wherever silence goes, reflection follows.

The puddles still; their surfaces compose
the clouds, the monks, the street—the art of time.
The bell rings twice because the bell is hollow.
Wherever silence goes, reflection follows.

Harvest

Watch the golden wheat
undulate, wave after wave
the grasshoppers feast.

The Brief Kingdom of May

One little boy
petting my dog asks,
Why is he so soft?
Because he likes being soft,
answers his friend.

Beside us, the lilac bush
is purple because it
thinks of itself
as royalty, waving
to everyone
in the neighborhood
with one hundred
perfumed handkerchiefs.

Above us, the red-winged
blackbird singing
on the maple branch
adores arias,
imagines itself
in the spotlight
at the opera house.

At our feet, the worms
draw squiggly lines
on the sidewalk
because they cherish
calligraphy, and the broad
concrete expanse
is perfect for practicing
their curlicues.

All the while, the clouds
form and dissipate
overhead,

delighting in
impermanence,
as in childhood,
or a dog's life,
or the fleeting grace
of spring.

The Magician

wears
a cloak
of air

braids
waves

conjures
dunes
over here

that disappear
over there

bends
pines'
spines

juggles
seagull
osprey
eagle

whistles
high
through
a cloud's
agate
eye

whittles
the moon
down to
one bright
rind.

V.

Watching the Fox Disappear

Living Out West

becomes real to me
when the horses
I thought were painted
on the Wells Fargo
billboard step out
of the frame
and gallop past me
down the long hill
toward town.

Watching the Fox Disappear into the Shadow
of Saddle Butte

She turned on
a hum in the hill
like the pull
of sap in a tree
or the purr
of a pulse
in the blood.

Her gait skittery,
coat maple-brown
satin. The plume
of her tail rose,
fawn-colored smoke
over her shoulder.

She hugged
the downslope
as one might
brush sage
with her fingers,
sliding under the fence,
past the puzzled
horses, and into
the bone-white field.

She knew just
where to run—
a rusty key
in the half-light,
a quick twist of red—

Infinity, August, Bear Paw Mountains

How many clutches of cacti in the sun
or purple thumbs of clover,
or red beads knotted on yellow branches,
or grasshoppers popping up
from burst seedpods?
But look—the thin line
of dirt in front of us
divides golden buttercups
by purple roosterheads,
and one woman plus one man
minus a blue car
with Tennessee plates
we passed at the trailhead
are so far ahead of us
they are just figures scribbled
on the horizon, smudged
by the shadow fingers
of the high hills,
and we can walk all day,
singing out, or even shouting,
our voices rising exponentially
up the mountaintops, reaching
for the high white
of the cloud's erasures, but
the figures still recede
into the distance, like numbers
in a long sequence—
we may never catch them.

Escaped

The black-and-white dog
is well-kempt, well-fed,
free from home.
All day as I sit at my desk
by the window,
he runs by—first east,
then west, then back again,
tail lifted in joy. He checks
out the bushes, sniffs
at doorsteps, hovers
by mailboxes,
but he never stays for long.
He knows the enchantment
of movement, of paws
on concrete, on gravel,
on grass; he loves the thrill
of scaring up cats from the weeds
and scraping by fence posts.
Nothing can contain him,
not even his own happiness,
which lifts like a tuft of fur
in the wind and blows on.

Driving to Billings in the Rain

There is one road to follow.
No traffic. An antelope
shrugged in a ditch. Three horses
beneath an overhang,
two out in the sagebrush.
All signs predict danger:
Elk crossing. Falling rock.
Crosswinds. Loose gravel.
The only stop
a Country Mercantile
with handwritten price tags
on every candy bar.
The yellow dog, going blind,
bumps into a stack
of firewood as he rises.
Stoic ranch buildings,
red-faced, squat in silence,
while trailers circle up
around family secrets.
Not even a hint of Billings
just twenty miles out.
The headline in the paper:
The Rain Came, the needed rain,
and brought a flood.

April Blizzard

Forget the driveway, birdhouse, hedgerow,
all their lines have faded overnight.
The yard's a snow globe filling up with snow.

No grass or tulips, no pavers lined up in a row—
the clouds put them to bed; they're swaddled tight.
Forget the neighborhood. Even the windows

of the house across the street are swallowed
by the blizzard's swirling appetite.
The town's a snow globe filling up with snow.

Gone are the bridges, bank signs, silos,
even the mountains ringing all these sights.
Forget language, too, except the crows

that spill across the page, flying from no
margin to no margin, ink-blotting the paper-white
world, this snow globe filling up with snow.

Be slow to rise. In a world turned adagio,
the crows call out one note, wrong-but-right.
Forget your scheduled meetings. Really, what's to know?
Your head's a snow globe filling up with snow.

Dear Middle of Nowhere

If anyone asks me where you are,
I just say, *Thirty minutes
from Canada. Four hours
from Glacier. Seven hours
from what used to be Yellowstone.*

Do you find it's easier
to say where you are not?

When a train derailed
outside Chester, Montana,
the national news anchor
kept zooming in and zooming in
on Google Earth, trying to find
a landmark. A town.

It's here somewhere, he said,
as if he knew
what he was looking for.

You're easy to overlook,
but you are always there,
scraping the edge
of the Canadian border,
the serrated knife of US-2
teethed with Malta, Chinook,
and Havre, cutting through
the golden winter wheat,
forming perfect rectangles,
like picture postcards
sent with no return address.

Winter Haiku

1.

Still hugging the snow
under the oak, the doe's shadow
waits for her return.

2.

Slush-melt from the roof
smacks at the back of my neck
to keep me moving.

3.

From a full-color
catalog, my husband plucks
whole springtimes of hope.

Thirteen Ways of Looking at a Pinecone

Petrified artichoke;
miniature pineapple;
flowerless bud;
raccoon's shuttlecock;
scepter of seeds;
mosquitoes' drinking cup;
snout of the bear
that follows you home;
Fibonacci's dreamscape;
3-D mandala;
missile launched
by squirrel or owl;
nature's prayer wheel
hunted by children
with sap-sticky fingers;
many-tongued mantra;
tiny phoenix
opening its wings
in the fire.

Acknowledgments

Thank you to the literary journals and anthologies in which versions of these poems first appeared:

Chautauqua: "Rabbit Logic"
Drunk Monkeys: "The Quaint Seaside Village Will Never Be the Same"
Freeze Ray: "We Loved Them, and She Didn't"
From the Depths: "Endangered Species"
Funicular: "Driving to Billings in the Rain," "Infinity, August, Bear Paw
     Mountains"
Grand Little Things: "To My Children," "Isn't It Something?"
Great Lakes Review: "Falling Letters"
Heron Tree: "Goldfinches"
Ilanot Review: "Your Anxiety Crushes on Donald Sutherland's Character
     in *Backdraft*," "The Easy-Bake Oven Presages Disappointment"
Midwestern Gothic: "Everything is Corn"
Montana Mouthful: "Drop Risk"
Mud Season Review: "Make Your Anxiety Work for You," "Your Anxiety
     Joins the Cast of SNL," "Your Anxiety Books a VRBO"
New Plains Review: "What Gets to Me"
One Sentence Poems: "Living Out West," "Winter Haiku" (as "December")
Otis Nebula: "Post-Madonna, I Tried Not to Look Afraid," "Re: Meetings,"
     "I Used to Be a Roller-Coaster Girl," "They Said It Couldn't Be Done"
River Heron Review: "Seven Monks, Bodh Gaya, India," "Watching the Fox
     Disappear in the Shadow of Saddle Butte"
Storm Cellar: "Oh, Are You Supposed to Use a Knife?"
Tiny Seed Literary Journal: "Thirteen Ways of Looking at a Pinecone,"
     "At a Rest Area Outside Des Moines"
Whitefish Review: "Escaped"

"Ode to the Geode" appeared in *Waters Deep: A Great Lakes Poetry Anthology* (Split Rock Press, 2018).

Thank you also to Casey Knott and Cassandra Labairon for their suggestions on these poems.

About FutureCycle Press

FutureCycle Press is dedicated to publishing lasting English-language poetry in both print-on-demand and Kindle formats. Founded in 2007 by long-time independent editor/publishers and partners Diane Kistner and Robert S. King, the press was incorporated as a nonprofit in 2012. A number of our editors are distinguished poets and writers in their own right, and we have been actively involved in the small press movement going back to the early seventies.

Each year, we award the FutureCycle Poetry Book Prize and honorarium for the best original full-length volume of poetry we published that year. Introduced in 2013, proceeds from our Good Works projects are donated to charity. Our Selected Poems series highlights contemporary poets with a substantial body of work to their credit; with this series we strive to resurrect work that has had limited distribution and is now out of print.

We are dedicated to giving all of the authors we publish the care their work deserves, offering a catalog of the most diverse and distinguished work possible, and paying forward any earnings to fund more great books. All of our books are kept "alive" and available unless and until an author requests a title be taken out of print.

We've learned a few things about independent publishing over the years. We've also evolved a unique and resilient publishing model that allows us to focus mainly on vetting and preserving for posterity poetry collections of exceptional quality without becoming overwhelmed with bookkeeping and mailing, fundraising activities, or taxing editorial and production "bubbles." To find out more, come see us at futurecycle.org.

The FutureCycle Poetry Book Prize

All original, full-length poetry books published by FutureCycle Press in a given calendar year are considered for the annual FutureCycle Poetry Book Prize. This allows us to consider each submission on its own merits, outside of the context of a traditional contest. Too, the judges see the finished book, which will have benefitted from the beautiful book design and strong editorial gloss we are famous for.

The book ranked the best in judging is announced as the prize-winner in January of the subsequent year. There is no fixed monetary award; instead, the winning poet receives an honorarium of 20% of the total net royalties from all poetry books and chapbooks the press sold online in the year the winning book was published. The winner is also accorded the honor of being on the panel of judges for the next years competition; all judges receive copies of the contending books to keep for their personal library.

www.ingramcontent.com/pod-product-compliance
Lightning Source LLC
Chambersburg PA
CBHW052342090426
42741CB00029B/3206